Cambridge English Readers

Level 2

Series editor

Superbird

Brian Tomlinson

CAMBRIDGE
UNIVERSITY PRESS

CAMBRIDGE
UNIVERSITY PRESS

University Printing House, Cambridge CB2 8BS, United Kingdom

Cambridge University Press is part of the University of Cambridge.

It furthers the University's mission by disseminating knowledge in the pursuit of education, learning and research at the highest international levels of excellence.

www.cambridge.org
Information on this title: www.cambridge.org/9780521656085

© Cambridge University Press 1999

First published 1999
Reprinted 2015

Printed in the United Kingdom by Hobbs the Printers Ltd

A catalogue record for this publication is available from the British Library

ISBN 978-0-521-65608-5 Paperback

Contents

Part 1

Chapter	**1**	Superbird crashes in the desert	5
Chapter	**2**	Escape from Superbird	9
Chapter	**3**	The house	13
Chapter	**4**	The drawing of Superbird	17
Chapter	**5**	The journey back home	20

Part 2   *One year later*

Chapter	**6**	The return	27
Chapter	**7**	June's daughter	34
Chapter	**8**	Captain Lake	39
Chapter	**9**	The Superbirds leave again	46

People in the story

Radio Announcer: announcer for Radio News Today programme

Mary Mount: astronaut on Superbird

Sam Bridges: astronaut on Superbird

June: Mary's friend

Sheila: June's daughter

Captain Lake: Captain of Superbird 2

Major Jones: Captain of Big Bird

Part 1

Chapter 1   *Superbird crashes in the desert*

Good morning. Welcome to Radio News Today. Twenty years ago today Superbird crashed into a hill in the middle of a desert. Well, we all know that, don't we? We all read the news in the Daily Star that said five people died: Ford, Stone, Sands, Bridges and Mount.

But now I can tell you the good news. Only four people died! That's right! Mary Mount came back from the journey to that strange land on Superbird. She's sixty years old now. This morning they let me visit Mary Mount. This is the first time she has ever spoken about the journey and the crash in the desert. Here is a recording of our conversation:

Hello Mary. It's nice to meet you. How are you?

I'm OK. I'm feeling a little old, but I'm happy to be here. It's nice to talk to somebody new.

Today Mary, is July 4th, twenty years since the crash in the desert.

Is it really? Twenty years ago today? I knew it was a special day today.

Would you tell us about that journey twenty years ago?

Well, it's strange. I've been quiet all this time. Then they said I can speak to you. So, yes, I think I can remember. What would you like to know?'

Well, could you tell us about that night in the desert? What happened exactly?

Ah, that night. Yes, I can remember that night. We were flying over this strange new place. We were taking photos of lights. First, there were lots of lights below us, lots of lights all together. Cities of lights. Then there were no lights. Just dark. And then there was a very loud noise, thunder, and something hit Superbird very hard.

What was it?

I don't know what it was. We tried the radio. Nothing. Then the lights in the ship went out. There was another loud noise, more thunder, and then lightning in the sky. Then it became very quiet. Superbird's engines just stopped.

Is that when you crashed into a hill?

Well, Bill Ford tried to land Superbird on the sand first. In the desert. There was soft sand everywhere. We landed on the sand. But then Superbird bounced just like a ball. Once, twice, three times. That's when we hit the hill.

And that's when all the men died?

No. No. Not then. Not straightaway. Bill Ford and Steve Stone died when we hit the hill, yes. Alan Sands was hurt. He couldn't move. But Sam Bridges and I were OK.

I looked out of the window of Superbird, but I couldn't see anything. No lights; just darkness. Everything black. Sam and I were afraid. We held hands.

'Let's go outside,' Sam said. 'Let's get away from the ship before they come.'

Who was he talking about?

I didn't know. I couldn't see anybody outside. I said, 'What about Alan?' Alan heard me and he said, 'You must go. Now. Go now before they come.'

Did you leave Alan Sands on Superbird?

Yes. We had to choose. We gave Alan a drink and then we left him on the floor. We opened the door of Superbird and went outside. We walked down the hill.

Then we saw lights on the road coming towards us fast. There were lots of bright lights and a very loud noise.

What were they?

Cars and trucks. We could only see the lights. We stayed close to the ground. We were hoping the lights would go on past us. But they stopped near the hill. Then there were lots of people and lots of noise, people shouting at each other. They put a light on Superbird. I could see Alan inside Superbird. He was looking out of the window.

Did they see you?

No. We were in the dark and they were all looking at Superbird.

Then somebody shouted and a lot of them ran up the hill. Some of them went inside Superbird. I could hear guns. They shot Alan. I could hear him shouting, screaming. He couldn't escape. They shot him three times; three shots. Then everything was quiet.

What about you? Did you have guns?

No. We had nothing. We stayed near the ground in the sand and watched from the dark. Then they came out of Superbird. They were carrying bags. Three bags. Ford, Stone and Sands. Then some of the lights went away, along the road, taking the bags. But some of them stayed on the hill. They were watching Superbird. But they couldn't see us.

Chapter 2   *Escape from Superbird*

What happened next?

We just stayed there in the dark, waiting. We were afraid and we held hands. We waited for a long time. Then more lights came from the dark with a lot more people and a lot more noise. They put Superbird on a truck and then they tried to drive it away into the dark.

But Superbird was very heavy and the truck stopped in the sand lots of times. At last they drove it away. It became very quiet again. There were still a few people and some lights but we couldn't hear any noise.

Could you see the people?

We were a long way away. But some of them were sitting under the lights and they looked very big, much bigger than us. We were afraid but we decided to move towards the lights to look at the people. We soon got close to the people.

What did they look like? Did they look like us?

No. Not at all. They were very tall. They had brown hair all over their heads and they had something in the middle of their faces. Like our noses but much bigger. And some had things over their eyes, things which came from their ears. Some had hair on their faces too.

Did they wear clothes?

Yes, they did, brown clothes. But not like ours. The clothes covered their bodies, they covered their arms, their legs and even the tops of their heads. And they wore guns.

But one of them was different. It had very long yellow hair right down its back. And it didn't have a gun. It was sitting. A very big brown-haired person was standing, talking to it.

Could you understand what they were saying?

I could hear them clearly. But the sounds were strange. The words were not the same as ours. The brown-haired one was very loud. It was shouting. The yellow-haired one was quieter, saying something like 'sir'. Over and over.

Did they see you?

Well, we stayed in the dark listening. Then there was a loud noise and the sky was full of light. The people saw us. They shot at us with their guns. We got up and ran back into the dark very fast.

They ran after us, shooting their guns. Now the sky was dark again and I ran up the hill. When I got to the top of the hill I stayed near the ground. Sam ... Sam didn't run up the hill. He ... he ran the other way, into the desert. They saw him ... He couldn't escape ...They shot him.

Are you OK?

Yeah, yeah, I'll be OK. I am very sad when I think of Sam. I liked Sam very much. I still think of him all the time.

Do you want to stop? We can talk again later.

No, no, I'm all right now. Where was I?

You were telling me about Sam Bridges.

Yes, that's right. They shot him four or five times. He fell down and they shot him again. They put their lights on his body and one of them said, 'No blood'. Something like that. And the others all said something like, 'Wow!'

Did they find you?

No. They looked for me everywhere with their lights but they didn't come up the hill. After a long time they went back to their cars and trucks and some of the cars drove away. Then I fell asleep.

How long did you sleep?

I don't know. But when I woke up the sky was not so dark. I could see a big red light in the sky, a long way away. Then I moved along the ground on my hands and knees to the top of the hill and down the other side. Then I ran away from the red light. It became lighter and lighter and the sky changed from black to blue. I ran and ran and then I saw a house. When I got near the house I saw lots of small people. They were all white, except one which was black; and they had four legs. They were eating something green in the sand. When they saw me they made strange noises and ran away towards the house. I ran too, towards the house.

Why? Why didn't you run away from the house?

I don't know. All I knew was that I wanted to run away from the light; I was afraid and tired and the house was dark. But it got lighter and soon the sky was blue and there was a yellow sun in the sky.

Chapter 3 *The house*

What happened when you got to the house?

Oh well, when I got to the house I looked through an open window and I could see one of the big people. It was one of the people with yellow hair, like the one which was saying 'sir'. This one had no clothes on at all and it was sitting in water. Its body was wet and very white. I could hear it singing through the open window.

Did it see you?

Not at first. But then another person, a person with four legs ran towards me. This one was brown and small; and it had long hair. It shouted very loudly in a strange voice. It wasn't friendly. The person in the water looked up and saw me through the window. It screamed very loudly and I screamed very loudly too. The four-legged person ran away. Then we were silent. We didn't scream anymore. I smiled at the yellow-haired person and it smiled at me.

Was it still in the water?

Yes, it was. But then it got out of the water, put on a white coat and it came outside the house to meet me. We looked at each other for a long time and then it touched my hand. Its hand was still wet but it was soft like Sam's hand the night before. We held hands and then it took me inside the house.

What happened in the house?

We went into a big room and sat down on chairs at a table. The four-legged person came back. The other one spoke to it quietly and it sat down near my feet and was very friendly.

Did they speak to you?

The four-legged one did but the yellow-haired one said nothing. It just smiled and held my hand. Then the yellow-haired one gave me something to eat. It was brown and flat and it was inside something which was white. The yellow-haired one put something red from a bottle on top of the brown thing and then smiled at me again. It also gave me a drink, a sort of cold, brown drink. I ate some of the food, drank some of the drink and tried to smile too.

What did it taste like?

I thought it might be dangerous to eat, but it was OK.

What happened after you ate the food?

The yellow-haired one took me into another room and put me into a bed. I lay down with my head on something white and soft. It put its mouth on my face. Then it left the room and the smaller person jumped onto the bed and went to sleep with me. When I woke up the big one was standing by the bed smiling. It was wearing a long red thing but I could see its legs. It gave me a newspaper just like the Daily Star. There were lots of words, which I couldn't understand, but there were also two photos.

One photo was of Superbird on the hillside. The other one was of Sam and myself with the lightning behind us in the sky. The yellow-haired person pointed to the photo of me and then pointed to me. Again it smiled.

What did it do with the photo?

It gave it to me. It cut the photo out of the newspaper and gave the photo to me. It put its finger on Sam in the photo and I started to cry. We both cried then and the four-legged one started to shout again. I've still got the photo. Here it is, I've never shown it to anybody before. You are the first person to see it.

It's not clear now, the paper is yellow. But I can see it's very important to you. Take care of it.

I will. It's my only photo of Sam.

Were there other people in the house?

No, there was nobody else in the house. Just the two of them. There were many small people outside, the white people I saw before, but there were no other people in the house. For three days there were no other people in the house. But I did hear a car one night and voices came and then went away. For three days I stayed in bed, often with the small one lying next to me, licking my hands and sometimes my face. Every night the yellow-haired person put its mouth on my face and then went away. Every morning when I woke up it was standing by my bed smiling.

Chapter 4   *The drawing of Superbird*

What happened after the three days?

When I woke up on the morning of the third day, the yellow-haired person was standing by my bed. It was smiling. It put its mouth on my face and then held my hand. I saw then that it had only five fingers on each hand. It pulled me gently out of the bed and took me into another room. In this room there were four very big people with brown hair and brown clothes sitting on chairs. They all had guns but they smiled at me and I smiled back at them. They took me to a car and put me in the back seat with the yellow-haired person. It held my hand while one of the brown-haired people put something over my eyes so that I couldn't see. Everything was dark again. I could hear the four-legged person shouting outside the car.

Where did they take you?

I don't know. When the car stopped somebody put their mouth on my face and got out of the car. Then the car moved again just a little way. When it stopped this time, somebody took my hand and pulled me gently out of the car. We walked for about two hundred metres and then stopped. They took the thing off my eyes and I could see that I was in a room. It was a nice room – very big and colourful. There were three brown-haired people there. They smiled at me and then we all sat down at a table.

Did you have something to eat?

No, not this time. They showed me a photo of Superbird on the hill after the crash, and they gave me a pen. At first I didn't know what they wanted me to do, so I just took the pen and smiled at the people. Then one of them started drawing Superbird with a pen on a piece of paper. Suddenly I knew what to do. I drew a picture of Superbird as it was before the crash. Then they all smiled too.

But, of course, I made mistakes in my drawing. I didn't draw the real Superbird. I drew ten windows not eight windows and I drew only one door, not two doors. I also drew the wrong shape.

Did they know that you were making mistakes?

Not at first. But then one of them stopped smiling. It took the drawing from me and looked at it carefully. Then it started shouting at me very loudly and it took out its gun.

What did you do? Were you afraid?

Very afraid. I threw the pen at the person with the gun and I ran out of the room.

Did they run after you?

No, they just shouted.

Did they shoot at you?

No, they didn't. I ran out of the room. I went through a big door and into a garden. There was nobody there. Just me and some trees.

Nobody ran after you?

No. I stopped and looked around. There was a high wall around the garden and I saw a door at the end of the wall. The door was open, so I quickly walked towards it. I went through the door and then saw the yellow-haired person standing on the road. It smiled at me, walked over to me, held my hand and then took me back through the gate, through the garden and back to the room.

Why didn't you try to run away?

I don't know. I think because it was my friend. It was always nice to me. The three brown-haired people were still sitting round the table. They just smiled at me when they saw me. They gave me the pen again and another piece of paper and they watched me as I drew. This time I drew a picture of the real Superbird.

I understand. How long did you stay there?

In the room?

No, I mean on the planet Earth.

A long time. Maybe nine months. I lived with the yellow-haired person. It told me its name was June and that it was a woman. She was very kind to me and we were good friends. She taught me their language. It's called English. And I taught some of them our language too.

Chapter 5   *The journey back home*

So tell us, Mary, how did you get back here? How did you get home?

After we learnt to speak to each other the people from Earth told me they wanted to take me home. And I wanted to come home. But we had to re-build Superbird first. I helped them. Then I taught them how to fly it.

Late one night, June came to my room with the four-legged person (it was called a dog; its name was Shep) and a lot of brown-haired people, who were all men. She put her mouth on my face while someone took a photo. Then she started to cry. I asked her why she was crying, but she didn't speak. She just turned round and left the room, still crying. I could hear Shep shouting as they put the thing over my eyes and took me to a car. Then they drove very fast and for a long way. When the car stopped they took the thing off my eyes and I could see Superbird.

When I got into Superbird I saw two brown-haired people wearing brown clothes. Their names were Jim and Steve and they told me that they were going to take me home. The three of us smiled and held hands as Superbird took off. I was sad when I thought of Sam. And of Ford, Stone and Sands. And I was sad when I thought of my friends in the house in the desert. But I was also very happy because I was going home.

Something happened when you got back here, didn't it?

Yes. That's right ... the journey back was fine. Then Jim and Steve told me to land Superbird in a desert at night. So I landed it in the middle of the Dark Desert.

Jim and Steve were not very friendly. They didn't smile. They got out their guns and told me to get into the small Supercar which was near the back door of Superbird. They opened that door and then got into the back seat of the Supercar.

They told me to drive the car off Superbird and into the desert. Then they told me to drive towards the hills. It was very dark but with lightning in the sky; just like the night when we crashed on Earth nine months before.

They told me to drive without lights; so I drove very slowly.

Were you afraid?

Well, yes, I was. I thought about what they did to Sam Bridges and to Alan Sands. I knew they could be dangerous. I didn't want to hurt them. But I thought they were going to kill me. It was very easy in the dark to start the Hiss machine. I just pressed the button under the radio. They didn't know about that. There was a small noise as the gas came out. They screamed for a short time and then they were dead.

What about you? What about the gas?

I was all right. The gas we used kills people but it doesn't hurt us.

But they made the new Superbird on Earth. Why didn't they know about the gas?

They took the Supercar from the old Superbird. It was OK. They just put it in the new Superbird. I didn't tell them about the gas. I don't really know why. It didn't seem to be important.

What happened next?

I put the car lights on and then I drove back to Superbird. I didn't know where I was exactly so I put all the lights on and waited for somebody to come. Soon a plane landed and four soldiers ran towards me with guns. I stood in the light waving my arms and shouting my name. Somebody shot a gun but it missed me. Then somebody shouted, 'Don't shoot. It's Mary Mount. She's come back.'

But why did they tell us you were dead? Where did you go?

The soldiers took me to a hospital and they asked me lots of questions. Every day for six months they asked me questions. They wanted to know all about the Earth people.

They wanted to know what I told the Earth people. I told the soldiers everything, just like I'm telling you. I told them about the drawings of Superbird I did for the Earth people and how I helped them build Superbird again. They became angry. They left me here all these years. I have been growing old in a small room with a soldier outside the door. And then today they opened the door and I walked out into the garden. And you were sitting there, smiling at me. Why?

Why what?

Why have they locked me in a room all these years? And why have they let me out now?

I don't know. What do you think?

I think they didn't want me to tell people about my visit to Earth. Maybe they didn't want me to talk about how Sam died or about the brown-haired people who came back with me on Superbird.

But why?

Maybe they want people here to feel friendly towards people on Earth. Or maybe they didn't want me to talk about my friends on Earth because they want people here to feel angry towards people on Earth. I don't know . . .

*   *   *

Ladies and gentlemen that's where the recording of my conversation with Mary Mount finished. A soldier who was watching us came over. He said his name was

Captain Lake. He told me to turn my tape recorder off. We asked him why we had to turn it off. He said he could not tell us. But he did say that, in the next twenty-four hours, they were going to Earth again for the first time in twenty years. Captain Lake then asked Mary Mount to go to Earth with them because she speaks English and because of her experience on Earth.

Mary said she was happy to return to Earth after such a long time. At this moment Mary Mount is with the other astronauts preparing to travel to Earth. There are five Superbirds going to Earth. She also told me she will be happy to speak to me on the radio when she returns from her second journey to Earth.

So, Mary Mount, if you are listening: have a safe journey and we look forward to talking to you when you return.

Part 2

One year later

Chapter 6 *The return*

Good morning. Welcome to Radio News Today.

We are here 'live' at the place where the Superbird spaceships are about to land. There is a big crowd here to meet Mary Mount, Captain Lake and the other astronauts. There are people in cars, people sitting on seats, people everywhere. The atmosphere is fantastic. There are hundreds of photographers here. And all over the world people are watching on TV. And here on Radio News Today, soon after the Superbirds land, Mary Mount is coming to speak to us about her second journey to the planet Earth.

Mary Mount left on Superbird 2 from here but is returning on a spaceship they built on Earth. It is called Big Bird. Everyone here is waiting to see what Big Bird looks like. The news reports in The Daily Star say that there are human beings on the ship and everyone is very interested to see what Earth people look like too.

And here they come now. And there is Big Bird. Big Bird looks similar to Superbird, but much bigger. All the people are very excited. They are shouting and calling. But the noise of Big Bird is much louder than the people shouting. It's just landing now, and any moment we'll be able to see Mary Mount and the other astronauts come out of Big Bird.

The door is opening. Everybody is shouting and cheering. And there is Mary Mount. And with her is an old man. They're holding hands. People are shouting and smiling and taking photographs. And here are some humans.

Everyone is waving to them now. And here come the other members of the crew. Mary Mount is going back into the ship. She's bringing out an animal. It's a dog, I think. They're all standing in front of the spaceship now, waving to the people, shouting 'hello', smiling. I can't see Captain Lake at this moment.

Hundreds of photographers are taking photos for newspapers and magazines. And all over the world people are watching on TV. They are watching two people from different worlds holding hands. It's a fantastic moment. All the astronauts are getting into cars now. And very soon we are going to speak to Mary Mount about her journey to Earth . . .

* * *

And, as we promised, here now is Mary Mount. Hello Mary?

Hello. How are you?

Fine. What about you? You must be tired after such a long journey?

Yes, a little, but I'm fine.

Can you tell us your story about the journey?

Sure. What would you like to know?

Well, we saw that Captain Lake was not with you. Where is he? Is he all right?

Well, Captain Lake is still on Earth. He's in prison.

In prison?

Yes, in prison. It's a long story...

Well, we would all like to hear that story.

Well ... OK ... It all started with the flight to Earth. There were five spaceships. On my spaceship there were seven people altogether. There was Captain Lake and the other members, Hill, Forest, Woods, Home and Beach.

How did you feel about going back to Earth?

I didn't know what to feel. I was happy because I was going back to Earth where I had many friends. I was worried because of what happened twenty years ago with Jim and Steve.

Yes, I can understand. How long did the flight take?

Seven days. I slept a lot. And I had a lot of dreams about Earth. In my dreams I saw my friend June singing in the bath. I could also see Sam in my dreams and lights in the sky and guns killing Sam ... I became good friends with Sylvia Beach. I also spent a lot of my time with the others on Superbird 2. I told them about life on Earth and I taught them some English. I taught them to say 'hello' and 'please' and 'thank you', and I taught them lots of words like 'beer', 'coke', 'dollar' and 'bed'.

What do they mean? What do these words mean?

I'll teach you English if you like.

OK. Then maybe I can go to Earth.

Yes, all right. One strange thing about the journey to Earth was that Captain Lake didn't speak to me the whole journey. He was very quiet.

He never spoke to you?

Well, yes ... But only twice. The first time was on the last night. He asked me to tell him about the first crash in the desert again. He wanted me to tell him about Alan Sands. He said he was a good friend of Alan's. He looked angry when I told him how Alan died. I was worried that he would not be friendly to the humans.

Then, the next day, we looked out of the window and I saw that Superbird 2 was near the Earth. Captain Lake talked to me again. He asked me to speak in English with the people from Earth.

So while Superbird 2 flew round the Earth I spoke to the humans in English on the radio. The other four Superbird spaceships stayed away.

What did you say?

I said to the people on Earth: 'This is Mary Mount. I'm your friend. There are seven of us. We want to land. We want to be your friends. Can we land?'

'Why have you come back?' the humans asked me. 'Where are Jim and Steve? Are they with you?'

'No,' I said. 'They are not with us. I can explain when we land. We want to make friends with the people on Earth.'

The humans didn't want us to land at first. 'What about Jim and Steve?' the humans asked again.

'They're dead. I will explain everything when we land. I'm sorry they are dead. We want to be your friends.'

'We want to be your friends too,' the humans said.

We needed to land, so I said, 'We want to land in the desert. Is it OK for us to land?'

'OK. We'll meet you there. But please don't use any guns,' the humans said.

'We won't,' I said, 'we promise. Thank you.'

Then what happened?

Superbird 2 flew over the desert and I looked down on the night sky. This time there were no lights in the sky and no noise. Everything was black below us and everything was very quiet. Suddenly there was a very loud noise, the noise of guns. It was Captain Lake. He was shooting at the Earth. Then the sky was full of lights. It was the guns of the humans. They were shooting back at us.

What did you do?

I started shouting at Captain Lake: 'This is terrible. Don't shoot at the people on Earth. Stop!'

Did he stop?

No. Then there was a fire on Superbird 2. I looked out of the window as Superbird 2 tried to land in the desert. I saw all the soldiers and the guns and people running away from where Superbird 2 was trying to land. And I screamed when we hit the ground and then crashed into a hill.

'It's just like twenty years ago,' I thought. This time my leg hurt and my arm too. And then Superbird 2 was on fire. I remember I thought 'I must get out. I must get out . . .'

Chapter 7   *June's daughter*

How did you get out?

I don't know. When I woke up I saw I was in a bed and I heard people talking in another room. It was dark in the room and I couldn't see what was in there.

Did you get out of bed?

No. I couldn't get out of bed because of my leg. I just shouted, 'Hello! Where am I?' In the dark I could just see some people coming into the room. One of them put the light on. It was a man wearing a white coat. There was also a young woman who looked like June. She had yellow hair and long legs, just like June. And then I heard a dog shouting. They call it 'barking'.

A dog? In a hospital?

Well, it wasn't a hospital. And I knew the dog. 'Shep!' I shouted. 'Shep, come here.'

'It's not Shep,' said the young woman. 'It's Judd, the son of Shep.'

The dog came into the room and started barking at me.

'OK Judd. Be quiet!' said the young woman. 'This is Mary. She's our friend.'

The dog stopped barking and was friendly, just like Shep was.

Who was the woman?

It was the woman you saw arrive in Big Bird today. Her name is Sheila. She's June's daughter. She has the same colour hair, yellow, just like her mother's. And the same colour eyes. The first time I saw Sheila I thought it was June. Sheila said that her mother died a few years ago.

'I'm very happy to meet you,' Sheila said to me. My mother told me all about you. She talked about you all the time.'

'I'm happy too,' I said. But I was very sad about June … The man in the white coat was a doctor. He said to me: 'You're a very lucky woman, Mary. You're lucky to be alive. The spaceship was on fire when they pulled you out. You nearly died.'

What happened to the others, to the other people on Superbird 2?

Most of them died. Two of them were OK.

Who were they?

One of them was Sylvia Beach. She was the only woman. I was very glad that Sylvia was still alive.

You said it wasn't a hospital.

Yes, I suddenly became very tired and everybody left me alone to go to sleep. When I woke up it was light and Judd was on my bed. Then I knew I was in the same room that I slept in twenty years ago. I was back in the house in the desert where June and Shep used to live. I looked around the room. The pictures, the flowers and the bed were new. But it was the same old room and I was very happy to be back.

Were you still hurt?

My leg and arm still hurt, but I could walk. I had a bath in the same bath where I first saw June, where I saw June singing. Then I got dressed and went into the kitchen. There were two soldiers sitting at the table. They were wearing the same brown clothes the soldiers wore twenty years before. Sheila was sitting with them too.

'Good morning, Mary,' said one of the soldiers. 'How do you feel?'

'Good morning,' I said. 'I'm OK.'

'Good,' said the soldier. 'My name is Major Jones. We want you to help us.'

'To help you?' I asked. 'How?'

'It's very important. There are four Superbirds going round and round the Earth. We want you to talk to them.

We want you to tell their captains to land the Superbirds on Earth. We don't want to fight. We want to be friends.'

Was it true? Did they want to be friends?

I think so. But I said to Major Jones, 'You shot your guns at Superbird 2 first!'

'No, you shot at us first,' said Major Jones.

'Is that true?' I asked, 'Captain Lake shot at you first?'

'Yes, it's true,' he said. 'We didn't want to shoot.'

Why did Captain Lake shoot at them?

I think because he was still angry about what happened to his friend, Alan Sands, twenty years before. Or maybe he was afraid they would shoot at Superbird 2.

Did you help Major Jones?

Yes, I talked to the captains of the other four Superbirds and I told them that it was OK to land. I told them that the Earth people wanted to be our friends.

Did you tell the people on the other four Superbirds about what Captain Lake did, the people he killed, and about the crash.

No, I didn't.

Did they ask about the crash?

Yes. They saw the crash on the television screens. I told them we were OK.

Why?

I didn't want them to be afraid. I wanted them to land and to make friends with the Earth people.

Did they land?

Yes. In the afternoon the four Superbirds landed in the desert. I went with Sylvia Beach to meet the crews as they came out of their spaceships. There were lots of soldiers there but no guns. The soldiers were smiling and friendly and they helped the crews to get into cars. They took them to a hospital in the desert to make sure they were OK. I went with them to the hospital so that they could look at my arm and leg and so that I could talk for the crews.

Did you stay in the hospital?

No. I wanted to stay with Sheila and Judd. But every morning a soldier drove me to the hospital to see the doctor about my arm and my leg and to talk to the crews. Every afternoon they drove me back to Sheila's house. This happened for a week. One afternoon when I came back to the house there was the soldier, Major Jones, sitting at the table drinking coffee with Sheila.

What did he want?

He said I had to go somewhere with him. He wanted me to answer some questions.

Chapter 8   *Captain Lake*

'Did you know about the guns?' Major Jones asked me.

'I saw them on the ship. I wasn't happy about the guns.'

'I'm not happy either. Ten of our soldiers died.'

'I'm sorry,' I said. 'That's terrible, I didn't want anybody to die.'

What did Major Jones say then?

He said, 'Mary, I want you to come with me to see Captain Lake.'

'What?' I said. 'He's dead. He died in the crash.'

Was he dead?

No, he wasn't dead, he was in the hospital. He was OK. 'We want you to talk to him,' Major Jones said. 'We want you to tell him to say he's sorry he shot his guns at us. Then there will be no more fights and we can all be friends.'

Did you talk to Captain Lake?

Yes, I went with Major Jones to the hospital. First of all we went to see Sylvia Beach to ask her to help us and then all three of us went to see Captain Lake. He was in a small room. It had just a bed, a chair and a very small window above the door. Outside the door there was a soldier with a big gun.

Major Jones stayed outside the room while Sylvia and I talked to Captain Lake. We talked to him for about thirty minutes. At first he was very angry. He said that they killed Alan Sands and he was going to kill them. We told him that the Earth people were good to us, that they really wanted to be our friends.

What did he say then?

He didn't say anything. He just listened to us without speaking for a long time. Then suddenly he smiled and said, 'OK. I'll say I'm sorry.'

When we came out of the room we were smiling. When Major Jones saw us he went straight into the room and after a few minutes he came out with Captain Lake. A soldier brought a microphone and another soldier brought a television camera. Captain Lake looked into the television camera and spoke very slowly into the microphone. He said the words which I told him to say.

'I am sorry. I was wrong. I shot my guns at your . . .' He looked at me for help.

'Soldiers, at your soldiers,' I said.

'I shot my guns at your soldiers. I fired my guns first. I was wrong. I am sorry. I am sorry.'

Was everybody happy?

All over the Earth, people watched Captain Lake saying he was sorry. And then on the television we saw the President of the United States. From the White House in Washington the President talked to us.

'That's good,' he said. 'Thank you, Captain Lake. We can be friends now. I want to meet you and Mary Mount. Please come to Washington to stay with us in the White House.'

Did you go to Washington straight away?

No. I went back to Sheila's house. When I got back to the house there was somebody drinking coffee with Sheila. It was one of our people but it wasn't one of the crew and he seemed to be old. He was looking away from the door so I couldn't see his face.

'Hello,' I said. 'Do I know you?'

'I think you do,' said the man, as he turned round to look at me.

'Sam! Sam! It's you. I thought you were dead. This is wonderful. I'm so happy.'

It was Sam? Sam Bridges? He was still alive?

Yes, it was Sam. He looked at me for a long time and then he said, 'I'm not dead. They didn't kill me. I was in the hospital for a long time but I'm all right now. Mary, you look great.'

'Sam, I'm so happy. I don't know what to say.'

'Well, just kiss me then and make me happy too.'

'Kiss you? How? I don't know how to kiss you.'

'I'll show you. Come here.'

What did he do? What does 'kiss' mean?

He put his mouth on my mouth, just like June did. It was very nice. We sat together at the table and talked for a long time about the last twenty years. We talked in English so Sheila could understand and sometimes she told us about her mother, June.

Sam told us that he worked for the soldiers and that he was helping them to make ships like Superbird. He lived in the hospital and this was the first time he had been in the desert in twenty years.

What about the President? Did you go to Washington?

Yes. All over the world people watched on television as the President talked to Captain Lake and myself. The President told us we were his friends. He told us we could stay in America as long as we wanted to and we could go anywhere we liked.

Was Captain Lake happy now?

I thought he was. He was smiling all the time at the President. But then I saw him looking angry. And then I saw a very small gun in his hand. I ran towards him shouting, 'No, don't do it! No!' I got to him just as he tried to shoot the President. I pushed his arm as he shot the gun. The bullet hit the President but fortunately it hit him in the arm.

What happened to Captain Lake?

He ran out through a large window into the garden as many soldiers shot their guns at him. Then he got into a car

and tried to drive it very fast. But it was difficult to drive and the soldiers shot at the car and the car crashed into a gate.

Was Captain Lake OK?

Yes. But the soldiers took him away. It was on television many times that night, Captain Lake shooting the President and then crashing into the gate.

What about you? Were you OK?

I was OK, but I was very angry with Captain Lake. It was a very stupid thing to do. He nearly started a war between our people and the Earth people. I said to the President, 'I'm sorry. I'm sorry. He's a stupid man'.

Is Captain Lake the reason you came home?

No. The President is a good man. He said he still wanted to be our friend. He wanted us to talk to the people of Earth, to tell them that we were their friends. We went to London, to Paris, to Rome, to Tokyo, to Sydney and to Singapore. We gave talks on television and we told the people of Earth about our world. But most of the time I stayed with Sam at Sheila's house in the desert. Major Jones often came to the house, at first to talk to us, but also to see Sheila.

Did you go to see Captain Lake?

No. I didn't want to see him again. I knew he was never going to say sorry. I saw him on television sometimes, always with lots of soldiers holding him. But I didn't want to speak with him.

What about Sylvia Beach and the others who came on the Superbirds? What happened to them?

They all learnt English and then they travelled around the world too. Sometimes they taught people about our world and sometimes they learnt about life on Earth. They learnt many new things: how to play jazz, how to make beer, how to swim and how to play football. And they taught people how to 'jample' trees and how to play 'splert'. They also made many friends.

Does everybody on Earth speak English?

No. There are many languages. We learnt some French, some German, some Spanish, some Italian and some Japanese too. But many people speak two languages and you can speak English to people in most places in the world.

People were sad when they heard the President say on television that the Superbirds were ready to fly home. Major Jones was going to fly the new American Big Bird with the Superbirds. Sam and I were going to fly with Major Jones on Big Bird and Mrs Sheila Jones was going with them too.

Mrs Sheila Jones?

Yes. Sheila and Major Jones got married.

Were you happy to be coming home?

Yes. But we were also sad too. On the morning of the flight we said goodbye to the house which was also our home. We looked for Judd to say goodbye but he wasn't there. When the car came for us we looked one last time for Judd, but we couldn't find him anywhere.

Chapter 9 *The Superbirds leave again*

Did all the Superbirds take off together?

Yes. And Big Bird too. When the ships took off thousands of people were there in the desert to shout goodbye and all over the world people watched on television. As we took off from Earth, I held hands with Sam and Sheila on Big Bird and we watched out of the windows as the Earth became very small below us.

After we took off we heard a noise. It was barking. It was Judd the dog. He got on Big Bird when no-one was looking. Major Jones was not happy, but when Sheila smiled at Major Jones and held his hand he said it was OK.

And what about the flight back. How did you spend your time?

I spent the flight in a very similar way to the flight to Earth a year ago. I taught our language to the American crew, I thought a lot about Sam and I often went to sleep. But this time most of my dreams were good. I saw blue skies, happy faces and a very happy dog. There was one dream though which was very bad. In it I saw a huge black thing in the sky and below it many people were dying. I heard them shout, I heard them scream and I saw them die. But when I woke up I looked around and people were smiling and happy and I was with Sam and our dog. I talked to Sam about our life together. After so many years away from each other and after so many years living alone in a small room, we both want to have a nice house and to do things together. We want to do some of the things which we enjoyed doing together on Earth. We want to go for walks with Judd, to watch television, to play music, to read good books.

Are you happy now Mary?

Most of the time I'm very happy. But sometimes I see the black thing from my dream. I told Sam about it but he just said that everything was going to be OK.

Well, Mary. You're home now . . .

What's that noise?

I don't know, Mary, but everyone is looking at the sky.

What are those black things? Are they spaceships, new Superbirds?

I'm not sure. I think so. It looks like they are going to take off. Mary, where are you going? . . . Well, Mary has left the studio, ladies and gentlemen. She seems very worried. There is a strong wind now. The black space ships are going to take off. There is a lot of noise.

I can see Mary Mount now. She is talking to a soldier. She is shouting at him. The black spaceships are in the sky now. They are probably going to Earth. But why? Are they going to Earth to get Captain Lake? Mary Mount looks very angry. People are taking photographs of the spaceships as they take off. There's a lot of noise and confusion. I can see Sam with Mary now. They are talking. Sam is shaking his head. They both look very sad now as they watch the black spaceships getting smaller in the sky. The crowd are quiet now. Everything is quiet. Mary and Sam are

holding hands. They are walking with some soldiers towards a car that is waiting to take them to their new life. I hope everything is going to be OK ...